Local Government
BOARD
BUILDERS

How Are We Doing? Evaluating Manager and Board Performance

Second Edition

Kimberly L. Nelson

School of Government

The School of Government at the University of North Carolina at Chapel Hill works to improve the lives of North Carolinians by engaging in practical scholarship that helps public officials and citizens understand and improve state and local government. Established in 1931 as the Institute of Government, the School provides educational, advisory, and research services for state and local governments. The School of Government is also home to a nationally ranked Master of Public Administration program, the North Carolina Judicial College, and specialized centers focused on community and economic development, information technology, and environmental finance.

As the largest university-based local government training, advisory, and research organization in the United States, the School of Government offers up to 200 courses, webinars, and specialized conferences for more than 12,000 public officials each year. In addition, faculty members annually publish approximately 50 books, manuals, reports, articles, bulletins, and other print and online content related to state and local government. The School also produces the *Daily Bulletin Online* each day the General Assembly is in session, reporting on activities for members of the legislature and others who need to follow the course of legislation.

Operating support for the School of Government's programs and activities comes from many sources, including state appropriations, local government membership dues, private contributions, publication sales, course fees, and service contracts.

Visit sog.unc.edu or call 919.966.5381 for more information on the School's courses, publications, programs, and services.

Aimee N. Wall, DEAN
Jeffrey B. Welty, SENIOR ASSOCIATE DEAN FOR FACULTY AFFAIRS
Anita R. Brown-Graham, ASSOCIATE DEAN FOR STRATEGIC INITIATIVES
Willow S. Jacobson, ASSOCIATE DEAN FOR GRADUATE STUDIES
Kara A. Millonzi, ASSOCIATE DEAN FOR RESEARCH AND INNOVATION
Lauren G. Partin, SENIOR ASSOCIATE DEAN FOR ADMINISTRATION
Sonja Matanovic, ASSOCIATE DEAN FOR STRATEGIC COMMUNICATIONS
Matt Marvin, ASSOCIATE DEAN FOR ADVANCEMENT AND PARTNERSHIPS

FACULTY

Whitney Afonso
Gregory S. Allison
Rebecca Badgett
Julie Beasley
Maureen Berner
Kirk Boone
Mark F. Botts
Brittany LaDawn Bromell
Melanie Y. Crenshaw
Crista M. Cuccaro
Leisha DeHart-Davis
Shea Riggsbee Denning
Sara DePasquale
Kimalee Cottrell Dickerson
Phil Dixon, Jr.
Belal Elrahal
Rebecca L. Fisher-Gabbard
Jacquelyn Greene

Timothy Heinle
Cheryl Daniels Howell
Joseph L. Hyde
Colt Jensen
James L. Joyce
Robert P. Joyce
Diane M. Juffras
Joseph Laizure
Kirsten Leloudis
Adam Lovelady
James M. Markham
Christopher B. McLaughlin
Jill D. Moore
Jonathan Q. Morgan
Taylor Morris
Ricardo S. Morse
C. Tyler Mulligan
Kimberly L. Nelson

Kristi A. Nickodem
Obed Pasha
William C. Rivenbark
John Rubin
Dylan Russell
Meredith Smith
Daniel Spiegel
Carl W. Stenberg III
John B. Stephens
Elliot Stoller
Charles Szypszak
Shannon H. Tufts
Amy Wade
Teshanee T. Williams
Catherine Wilson
Kristina M. Wilson

© 2026
School of Government
The University of North Carolina at Chapel Hill

Printed in the United States of America
30 29 28 27 26   1 2 3 4 5
ISBN 978-1-64238-136-8

About the Series

Local Government Board Builders offers local elected leaders practical advice on how to effectively lead and govern. Each of the booklets in this series provides a topic overview, and many offer specific tips on effective practice, worksheets, and reflection questions to help local elected leaders improve their work. The series focuses on common activities for local governing boards, such as selecting and appointing committees and advisory boards, planning for the future, making better decisions, improving board accountability, and effectively engaging stakeholders in public decisions.

Kimberly L. Nelson, Distinguished Professor in public administration and government at the UNC School of Government, is the series editor.

Other Books in the Series

Strategic Planning for Elected Officials, Obed Pasha, 2025

Suggested Rules of Procedure for the Board of County Commissioners, Trey Allen, Fourth Edition 2017

Suggested Rules of Procedure for a City Council, Trey Allen, Fourth Edition 2017

Wicked Problems: What Can Local Governments Do?, Eric M. Reece and Maureen M. Berner, 2014

Handbook for North Carolina Mayors and Council Members, David M. Lawrence, 2013

Local Government Budgeting: A Guide for North Carolina Elected Officials, Julie M. Brenman with Gregory S. Allison, 2013[1]

---

1. Revised, updated edition planned by Gregory Allison and William Rivenbark.

The Property Tax in North Carolina, Christopher B. McLaughlin, 2012

Getting the Right Fit: The Governing Board's Role in Hiring a Manager,
Vaughn Mamlin Upshaw, John A. Rible IV, and Carl W. Stenberg,
2011[2]

Local Government Revenue Sources in North Carolina, Kara A. Millonzi,
2011[3]

Public Outreach and Participation, John B. Stephens, Ricardo S. Morse,
and Kelley T. O'Brien, 2011

Working with Nonprofit Organizations, Margaret Henderson, Lydian
Altman, Suzanne Julian, Gordon P. Whitaker, and Eileen R. Youens,
2010[4]

*Creating and Maintaining Effective Local Government Citizen Advisory
Committees,* Vaughn Mamlin Upshaw, 2010

A Model Code of Ethics for North Carolina Local Elected Officials,
A. Fleming Bell, II, 2010[5]

*Leading Your Governing Board: A Guide for Mayors and County Board
Chairs,* Vaughn Mamlin Upshaw, 2009

Be sure to look for new and revised editions available in 2026 and 2027.

---

2. Revised, updated edition planned by Julie Beasley and Carl Stenberg.
3. Revised, updated edition planned by Rebecca Badgett.
4. Revised, updated edition planned by Teshanee Williams.
5. Revised, updated edition planned by Rebecca Fisher-Gabbard.

Acknowledgments

This edition of *How Are We Doing? Evaluating Manager and Board Performance* builds on the previous version, authored by Vaughn Mamlin Upshaw and published in 2014.

Contents

Introduction

Creating a successful local government requires that the manager and the governing board develop and maintain a culture of mutual respect, trust, and responsibility. The governing board and the public manager are charged with meeting legal, ethical, strategic, financial, and public expectations. Together they decide what services will be offered, to whom they will be offered, and what the quality and cost of the services will be. Establishing a set of clear agreements about what the board and manager are responsible for and a system to evaluate both board and manager performance enables a board and its manager to identify areas of strength and opportunities for development.

Even though performance evaluations for municipal and county managers are voluntary in North Carolina, many governing boards conduct annual evaluations of their managers. Increasingly, local government managers request that the evaluation process be included in their contracts. Annual evaluations of the manager, attorney, and clerk are considered "best practice." Similarly, many governing boards perform *self-evaluations* not because the law requires it but because it improves the members' ability to work with each other as well as with the manager and staff.

Just as employees find it difficult to perform well with unclear expectations and limited feedback on their work, a governing board will struggle to operate without agreement on member expectations, roles, and responsibilities. When members of the board have contradictory agendas and struggle to find common ground, or if board members are in conflict (particularly if that conflict becomes personal), the organization's ability to succeed is affected. Professional public managers who work with governing boards that do not agree about priorities and lack professionalism in establishing policies tend to voluntarily leave their positions rather than work in a dysfunctional environment.[1] To reduce the likelihood of unmanageable conflict and its consequences, a governing body should review its own performance annually, in conjunction with either its strategic planning retreat or with the manager's evaluation process.[2]

There are many ways for boards to conduct performance evaluations. For a process to be effective, however, it is important to make sure that the approach used is appropriate for the people and circumstances involved. When a clear evaluation process is practiced on a regular basis, it is more likely that the board and manager will build strong, coherent goals for improving performance. Regularly conducting reviews also minimizes the chance that a review will be undertaken only in response to a crisis.

This guidebook describes best practices and offers practical tips for productively evaluating the manager's and governing board's performance. It provides examples of evaluation measures, rating scales, and formats along with suggestions for ongoing performance improvement. For those already doing performance evaluations for the manager or the board,[3] this guidebook offers suggestions that can strengthen an existing process. It may also be used as a step-by-step manual for developing a new evaluation process from the ground up.

---

1. Barbara C. McCabe et al., "Turnover Among City Managers: The Role of Political and Economic Change," *Public Administration Review* 68, no. 2 (2008): 380–86, https://doi.org/10.1111/j.1540-6210.2007.00869.x. Also see James B. Kaatz et al., "City Council Conflict as a Cause of Psychological Burnout and Voluntary Takeover Among City Managers," *State and Local Government Review* 31, no. 3 (1999): 162–72, https://doi.org/10.1177/0160323X9903100302.

2. Gus Morrison and Jan Perkins, "The Value of Going Back to the Basics," *Western City*, June 2005, 7–9. Also see Charldean Newell, "Enhancing the Governing Body's Effectiveness," chap. 3 in *The Effective Local Government Manager* (International City/County Management Association, 2004), 57–82.

3. People use different terms when referring to performance evaluations. Terms such as *performance review*, *annual review*, or *manager evaluation* are used interchangeably and refer to the same thing. In this publication, *performance evaluation* is used to cover all of these alternative terms.

Linking Levels of Accountability

Local governments face higher levels of scrutiny, particularly concerning financial practices, compared with other types of organizations. In North Carolina, there are several state agencies tasked with overseeing the finances and management of local governments, including the State Treasurer's office, which includes the Local Government Commission (LGC) and the State Auditor's office. Additionally, members of the public, staff, and the media expect municipal councils and county commissioners to demonstrate responsible financial oversight and ethical standards.

Accountability for the public good occurs through a series of interactions among a variety of partners. A governing board's accountability system should "seamlessly link one level of authority to another,"[1] establishing a shared line of sight for the community, organization, manager, and board. (See Figure 1.) A comprehensive accountability system ties the board's expectations for its own performance to expectations in other areas.

Improving accountability is difficult unless performance is monitored across levels in a complementary way. Each level of authority may have well-designed standards for performance, sound measurement systems, and good outcomes, but if expectations across levels are independent of one other, it is not an accountability system. Linking the governing board's accountability system to the one used for evaluating the manager's performance will help the board clarify goals for itself, the manager, and the organization. The governing board's strategic goals guide the public manager's annual priorities, and these priorities are used to establish departmental goals for employees, programs, and resources.

---

1. John Carver, "Accountability Isn't Blame: It's a System Characteristic," *Board Leadership* 2007, no. 93 (2007): 2.

Figure 1. Creating a Line of Sight for the Board

Accountability systems that include assessments of both the board and the manager also help boards and managers clarify how they share responsibility for achieving desired results. Publicly stating expected results and assigning responsibility for achieving them give elected and appointed officials, as well as the public, ways to monitor and measure change.

It is useful for an annual accountability cycle to be incorporated into the board's calendar. If an outcome is met or exceeded, the board can decide to adjust performance targets for the next cycle. If an outcome is not met, the board needs to understand why and determine what needs to be done to ensure a better outcome in the next cycle. Figure 2 illustrates a typical accountability cycle.

? Questions for Discussion

1. What might we do to make our governing board, manager, or organization more accountable?
2. What are the priority areas for developing line-of-sight accountability in our local government?

Figure 2. Annual Board Accountability Cycle

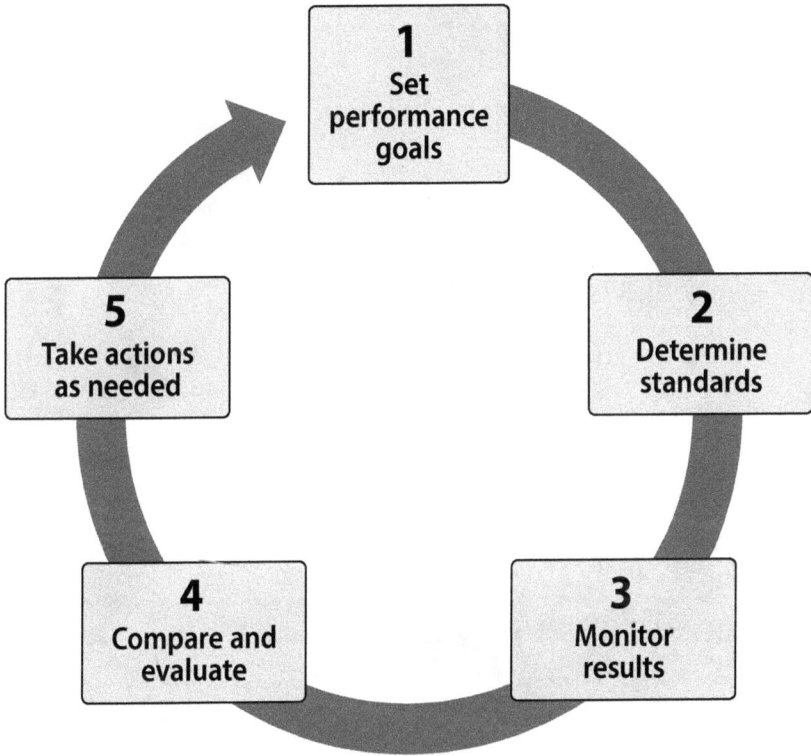

1 Set performance goals

2 Determine standards

3 Monitor results

4 Compare and evaluate

5 Take actions as needed

Manager Evaluation

In North Carolina, all one hundred counties have professional managers, and almost half of the state's municipalities employ full-time managers.[1] Although North Carolina statutes do not require municipal councils or boards of county commissioners to evaluate their managers, best practice suggests that governing boards should evaluate their professional managers at least once a year.[2] The majority of municipal and county managers expect to be evaluated by their elected boards on an annual basis. The following sections focus on assessing the manager's performance.

Why Should a Manager Request an Evaluation?

Lack of feedback can cause even the best managers to perform poorly. Without regular and effective feedback, managers may believe that they are doing what is expected, only to be reprimanded or fired for failing to meet an unstated expectation. Sometimes board members hear about something the manager has done indirectly or secondhand. Such information can cause board members to jump to conclusions about what the manager was doing and why. Without an opportunity to ask the manager directly about what has taken place, boards may perceive managers as having their own agendas. Regular performance evaluations give managers and board members an opportunity to clarify areas of misunderstanding and establish common goals.

---

1. In 2025, 48 percent of North Carolina's municipalities had full-time managers, and 83 percent of municipalities with populations over 2,000 employed full-time managers. UNC School of Government, Forms of North Carolina City Government database, www.sog.unc.edu/node/427.

2. David N. Ammons and Arnold Rodriguez, "Performance Appraisal Practices for Upper Management in City Governments," *Public Administration Review* 46, no. 5 (Sept.–Oct. 1986): 460–67.

A regular evaluation also allows a board to recognize and reward effective manager performance. Ideally, the evaluation process will also be linked to board decisions related to manager salary and benefits. Without a formal evaluation process, the justification for giving the manager a raise or taking other action may be questioned by members of the public. If someone asks why the manager was given a raise and the board has little or no justification, it may be difficult to defend the decision.

Some managers jokingly say that they do not need a formal performance evaluation because they are reviewed at every board meeting. Boards, however, rarely engage in conversations about manager performance as part of their regular meetings. Setting aside time for an annual evaluation provides an opportunity for the manager and the board to comprehensively discuss the manager's roles and responsibilities.

Scenario for Discussion

The city manager arrives for her annual performance evaluation feeling good about what she has accomplished over the past year. Following council policies, she maintained services without raising revenues by eliminating unfilled positions, collaborated with the economic-development director to recruit a new business that employs 150 people, and gained support from local contractors for a new ordinance that streamlines the approval process for new housing developments.

When the mayor asks the manager to reflect on her performance, the manager replies, "I think I've done well this year." Looking around the room, she notices that the council members are squirming in their chairs and casting sidelong glances at each other. "On no," she says to herself. "What am I missing?"

The mayor clears his throat and asks the council members to state how they think the manager has done. The first member says, "I know you have tried to do a good job this year, but there are still people in my district complaining about the lack of sidewalks and saying that the park needs upkeep." Another member chimes in, "Yes, and I still am waiting for you to respond to my request for a new website that can stimulate additional economic development."

The manager quickly realizes that her evaluation is not going as she anticipated. She says to the council, "I understand that you are frustrated because some of the things you asked for have not been done, but the issues you mentioned were not included in the budget or approved by the full council."

The mayor acknowledges the lack of full council approval on additional budget items but then says, "Citizens are complaining. I think it's time for the council to deliberate. Would you please step out? I will call you back in when we have a decision."

The city manager steps into the hall and takes a deep breath. "This was not what I expected," she mutters to himself. "I may need to start looking for a new job."

? Scenario Questions

- Why is a simple open question-and-answer session not an ideal method of performance evaluation?
- Why is it important that board members decide on a set of evaluation criteria to use to assess the manager ahead of time and share those criteria with the manager?
- Why is it not fair to hold the manager accountable for an inability to accomplish goals not approved by the full council?

Why Should a Board Evaluate the Manager?

An annual performance evaluation provides the board and manager a formal opportunity to review the manager's work over the previous year or other specified time period. Professional public managers are responsible for a variety of things, such as carrying out the governing board's directives, managing the local government organization, working with the public, coordinating activities with local business and community groups, and responding to unexpected crises as they occur. When boards take the time to regularly discuss how things are going, managers are able to offer the board more information about their work, and members of the board can make observations, offer advice, and provide feedback in a timely manner.

Conducting regular manager evaluations also allows board members to gain a better understanding of managers' challenges, particularly those that are outside their direct control. Sometimes, board members may think that a manager's inaction on an issue is because the manager is deliberately trying to circumvent the board's directives. In fact, the manager may have encountered unexpected challenges, such as a change in personnel that caused a delay, a regulatory requirement that held up progress on a new development, or an unexpected expense that required shifting resources away from the intended focus. Conducting regular evaluations provides the board and manager the opportunity to address such problems before they become entrenched.

?

Questions for Discussion

1. What does the manager expect from the evaluation process?
2. What do board members expect from the evaluation process?

What Constitutes a Good Evaluation Process?

A good performance evaluation is designed to provide feedback on a broad range of issues and to identify areas of strength and opportunities for development. It should address agreed-upon expectations from the manager's work plans as well as commonly expected standards for professional behavior and character. A performance-evaluation process should also have a standard structure and should be applied consistently over time. When performance evaluations are done infrequently, they are more likely to be used as a crisis-management tool to address a particular problem rather than as a way of assessing the manager's overall performance.

The evaluation should also be designed to provide an opportunity for the board and the manager to discuss options for reviving projects that were not completed. Such a conversation may lead to a revised work plan—perhaps one that puts greater emphasis on the things the manager controls directly or that increases the governing board's responsibility for making sure that the manager has the necessary support and resources to carry out the board's directives.

How Should the Manager's Performance Evaluation Be Conducted?

Although some governing boards delegate the evaluation to the board chair or mayor or to a subcommittee, the manager works for the entire board and should be evaluated by the full board. In a council–manager or county–manager form of government, the governing body appoints the manager to serve at its pleasure: Thus, the manager is responsible and accountable to the body as a whole.[3] Because individual members of the board may perceive a manager's performance differently, a performance review conducted by one person or by a subcommittee will not reflect the full board's perceptions.

Do All Manager Performance Evaluations Look Alike?

Performance evaluations come in a variety of shapes and sizes. The critical issue is finding the right approach for a particular situation. Since every manager and organization is unique, and the priorities for communities vary, there is no standard tool that can be used in every situation. There are, however, common features of good performance-evaluation instruments that can be tailored to reflect local needs and circumstances.

---

3. North Carolina General Statutes (hereinafter G.S.), Sections 160A-147 (municipalities) and 153A-76 (counties).

At a minimum, an evaluation should be designed to measure the manager's accomplishments during the year. Ideally, the manager and board have a common understanding about what the manager's priorities are and how success in those areas will be measured. To attain this, the board should convene a meeting with the manager at the beginning of the year (usually the anniversary of the manager's hiring) and develop a list of goals for the coming year. If the governing board has not adopted a plan at the beginning of the year, the manager can generate a list of priorities to address in the coming year and ask that the board include these in an evaluation instrument. If the manager generates the list of priorities, it is important that the board review that list and have the opportunity to discuss and make changes prior to incorporating them into the evaluation instrument. Without clear priorities, however, the manager's report may generate controversy because board members may have different ideas about what the manager should do. If the goals identified by the manager are inconsistent with those of the council, the manager may receive a positive evaluation by accomplishing the goals on the evaluation instrument, only to be fired later on for failing to address the board's unspoken priorities.

Scenario for Discussion

A manager operates without a formal work plan, but the governing board has clearly stated that it expects the manager to be responsive, to faithfully carry out board directives, and to operate the local government in an efficient and effective manner. During his evaluation, the manager reports that the annual survey of county residents showed broad satisfaction with county services, several new board policies were implemented, and the county government's financial outlook improved. The board members consider this information sufficient to allow them to fairly evaluate the manager's performance, and they give the manager a high rating.

? Scenario Question

What may be missed during this evaluation process?

The performance evaluation may also be designed to measure the manager's performance of routine, ongoing tasks such as communicating with the board, responding to members of the public, or improving technology within the organization. These activities are ones that most public managers are expected to undertake regularly, and they can be measured against agreed-upon standards. However, if the board and manager have not set measurable targets, there can be disagreement among board members or between the board and the manager over whether the manager has met expectations.

Scenario for Discussion

A town manager has an approved work plan that includes the development of a unified-development ordinance with the county, the creation of an economic-development strategy for a local industrial park, and the implementation of a new GPS app that allows residents to identify service needs. During the performance evaluation, the manager reports that the county governing board declined support for the ordinance, economic-development funding was eliminated from the annual budget, and the pilot for the app's implementation was not promising. The board conducts its evaluation and gives the manager a low rating based on the manager's failure to accomplish the goals set forth in the work plan.

? Scenario Questions

- Should managers be held accountable when factors out of their control lead to a failure to meet targeted goals?
- How can measures of a manager's efforts to accomplish goals be incorporated into a performance evaluation?

Professional practices and behaviors that influence a manager's effectiveness are often included in performance evaluations. This portion typically focuses on leadership skills and character traits that are essential to success in public management. Managers seek constructive feedback in these areas and benefit from it. However, because these traits are inherently subjective and thus harder to quantify, it is important for the board to clearly define key terms and establish measurable standards. For example, how does the board define *integrity*? What does *trustworthy* mean in this context, and how can these traits be assessed?

Finally, it is important to note that evaluations need to assess not only what has been accomplished but also how it was accomplished. For example, if a manager develops a consolidated purchasing system but neglects to include the people who will implement it in the planning process, the final system may be inefficient because important stakeholders were not involved from the outset. If the manager is evaluated on having completed the task but not on the way the task was accomplished, the evaluation may be positive, but the board may miss an opportunity to discuss issues critical to the manager's success. These types of questions may be difficult to incorporate into a written evaluation instrument. Ideally, the evaluation will consist of both a written instrument and a conversation about the manager's work.

What Constitutes a Good Evaluation Instrument?

Once the governing board and manager have agreed upon performance goals and expectations, the board needs to make sure that the evaluation instrument captures these components. A subcommittee of the board and the manager may work together to design an appropriate instrument.

It is important to design an instrument that is easy for the board to complete and yields feedback that the manager can understand. Instruments that have too many items, duplicate questions, or complicated instructions are difficult for board members and often provide confusing and inconsistent feedback to the manager. Also, poorly written or ambiguous questions can lead to difficult conversations and conflicting opinions among board members. Since every member of the board is expected to complete the evaluation, all members need to understand the questions and how the responses will be tallied.

Problems can arise if questions are included that ask board members to assess activities for which the board does not have an adequate basis for judgment. For example, the board does not receive detailed information about interaction between the manager and staff. If the board wants to evaluate staff satisfaction with the manager's performance, it should consider implementing 360-degree feedback.[4] However, using 360-degree feedback for a manager's performance evaluation alone is inadvisable for a variety of reasons. Most 360-degree-feedback instruments focus on generic leadership and management practices rather than the specific competencies required of a public manager. It is also inappropriate for a mixed group of respondents (including employees who report directly to the manager) to review a manager's performance when the manager works for and is ultimately responsible to the governing board.

Narrowly constructed items can be especially challenging for board members to assess. For example, asking board members to rate the manager's work with specific stakeholder groups or advisory committees may result in feedback based on hearsay or no feedback at all. If board members are unable to observe behavior and cannot accurately rate performance on an item, it is inappropriate to include that item in an evaluation instrument. Even if the instrument allows board members to indicate that they don't know how to rate the manager in a particular area, members may feel compelled to guess at the manager's competence. An evaluation that is incomplete or based on guesswork is not only unhelpful to the manager but may actually do more harm than good. Generally, if a majority of board members feel that they cannot accurately rate the manager on a particular item, the item should be eliminated from the evaluation instrument.

Incomplete or inaccurate responses are difficult for managers to interpret. Since local government boards are generally small, it will be difficult to interpret the board's assessment when there are divided results. Open-ended questions or an in-person meeting may help address some of these issues.

---

4. For professional management certification, the International City/County Management Association requires managers to complete 360-degree feedback every five years and a performance evaluation every year. The process involves self-evaluation along with feedback from a variety of sources, including the manager's supervisor, employees, and external clients.

Should the Manager's Performance Evaluation Be Standardized?

A thoughtful evaluation process can simultaneously track progress toward annual goals and document ongoing improvement in professional practice. Standardizing sections of a manager's performance evaluation provides information that can be compared over time. Some recurring items, such as preparing an annual budget, can be built into the performance evaluation each year. Other tasks, however, such as putting together a unified-development ordinance or a capital-improvement plan, may be unlikely to recur annually. Variable items provide feedback on activities that are time-dependent, while stable items offer input on areas associated with ongoing effective management. Varying items on the evaluation to accommodate changes in the manager's annual work plan may be appropriate at times, but changing the entire evaluation tool annually makes it difficult to measure the manager's progress.

What Can the Manager Contribute to the Evaluation Process?

The manager can begin by providing the board with examples of good performance evaluations. Managers typically know their responsibilities and priorities at work—job descriptions and professional standards detailing the common expectations for public managers are widely available. At the outset of the planning phase, managers can help their boards by preparing a list of priorities that they would like to have included in the evaluation. They can also identify practices relevant to accomplishing municipal or county goals. For example, in some areas it may be a priority for a manager to cultivate relationships with local media in order to ensure that the local government's concerns and perspectives are accurately represented. In other areas, the manager's focus may be on working closely with engineers and planners to ensure that infrastructure projects and new developments are designed and implemented in a manner consistent with board policy. In either case, it is important that the process reflect mutual expectations shared by the manager and the members of the board.

As part of the process, the manager should complete a self-evaluation using the same instrument used by the board. Often managers' impressions of their own performance differ from those of their boards. Even when a manager and board agree on the major goals for the year, a manager's work usually includes a variety of tasks beyond those identified as important in accomplishing the board's priorities. A manager also may have information about and insight into issues not listed on the annual work plan. When managers complete self-evaluations, they usually list achievements in other areas along with addressing progress on the previously identified priority goals. Many also include a narrative memorandum summarizing their overall activities and ongoing challenges. Ideally, the self-evaluation should give board members insight into both what the manager has achieved and how they perceive the quality and impact of their work.

Where Can the Manager and the Board Find an Example of a Performance-Evaluation Instrument?

The International City/County Management Association (ICMA) has developed a set of practices for effective public management that could be used as a starting point for a performance-evaluation instrument. (See Appendix A.) It lists and describes the performance expectations for an effective local government manager, but it is rare for any one person to be outstanding in every area listed. Depending upon the needs of the jurisdiction, the manager and board could agree on a subset of performance measures—usually five to ten—that they believe are critical for their local government. For instance, in a small jurisdiction where the manager wears many hats, the board and manager might decide that staff development should be a priority for the manager, while a larger organization with a stand-alone human resources (HR) department might decide that citizen participation should be a priority.

? Questions for Discussion

1. For a manager's first year in the position, are the board's expectations for the manager outlined in the manager's job description? If so, what are they? For subsequent years, are those expectations outlined in a set of annual goals presented to the manager?
2. What performance expectations need to be evaluated annually?
3. What expectations are variable and need to be evaluated only once or only once every few years?

Who Should Participate in the Manager's Evaluation Process?

Under North Carolina law, the local government manager works for the entire governing board—not an individual member, mayor, board chair, or subcommittee of the board. Therefore, the manager, the mayor or board chair, and all board members need to participate in the performance evaluation. Depending on the process agreed upon, there may also be roles for the clerk, the municipal or county attorney, the HR director, and an external facilitator.

The mayor or board chair often assumes a leadership role in the evaluation process. This may include initiating the process, helping draft an evaluation instrument, setting forth a process for the manager and board to follow, managing the performance-evaluation conversation, and working with the manager on specific issues following the performance evaluation. The mayor or chair can help ensure that an evaluation process succeeds by inviting the manager and board members to contribute their ideas about what is important to include in the evaluation. The mayor or chair may work with the manager and a subcommittee or external facilitator on an evaluation instrument that reflects the expectations of both the manager and the board. Because people are often uncomfortable giving and receiving feedback, the mayor or chair can lead by example by setting a positive tone and emphasizing the value of thoughtful performance reviews.

Should the Board Use an External Facilitator?

Someone trained to facilitate performance evaluations can be a great resource to the governing board and the public manager. Conversations surrounding performance evaluations are often difficult both for the individual receiving feedback and for those charged with providing a critique. Most people are unaccustomed to telling other adults what they do or do not like about the person's behavior or performance. Without someone to guide the process and the conversation, an inexperienced board can encounter surprises and challenges that the members may not be prepared to address. Additionally, in cases where a facilitator is not used, the local government may rely on the HR department to support the process. While it is acceptable for the HR department to distribute and collect the

Table 1. How a Facilitated Performance Evaluation Benefits the Manager and the Board

Manager	Board
Results in meaningful feedback	Professionalizes the process
Can identify hidden issues	Values all opinions
Separates message from the messenger	Makes the process easier
Focuses on opportunities	Improves clarity

Source: International City/County Management Association, *Manager Evaluations Guide* (ICMA, June 2025), 19–20, https://icma.org/documents/icma-manager-evaluations-guide.

instrument, given that the HR staff report to the manager, it is inappropriate for them to analyze or report on the results of the evaluation. See Table 1 for a summary of the benefits of using a facilitator.

How Should a Facilitator Be Chosen?

Facilitators should have experience working with governing boards and conducting performance evaluations for senior managers. The municipal or county HR director may be experienced in administering performance reviews within the organization, but the process used internally for department heads, supervisors, and professional staff necessarily differs from the process for the public manager or chief executive. Most organizations have job descriptions and performance objectives for internal positions that can be used as a basis for performance evaluations. However, public managers, like chief executive officers, often do not have clear-cut job descriptions and performance expectations; instead, their jobs may be outlined in a more general fashion. For example, a performance goal for the public manager might be "responsiveness to members of the public," but the manager would have substantial discretion in meeting this goal. An experienced facilitator can help design the performance-review instrument, work with members of the board and the manager to develop a plan for the session, analyze responses from the board and manager, and prepare a summary report for the performance-review session. A facilitator can also help the board and manager articulate performance goals and identify specific outcomes.

In addition to helping craft a meaningful evaluation tool, a facilitator can provide the following benefits.

Neutrality
Ideally, an external facilitator is someone who is trusted by both the manager and the governing board to provide fair and unbiased advice to all.

Full Participation
Using an external facilitator frees all members of the governing board to fully participate in the evaluation process. Without an external facilitator, the mayor or board chair is charged with running the meeting *and* providing feedback as a member of the governing board. It is hard to do both things well at the same time.

Establishment of Boundaries
Usually, a facilitator will talk to both the manager and the members of the board prior to implementing an evaluation process to make sure that all participants agree on goals for the evaluation and to get input on which issues are important to address. A good facilitator can also ensure that members of the governing board and the manager understand what will and will not be a part of the evaluation process. For example, if a board member attempts to use the evaluation session to chastise fellow board members for their lack of support on a particular issue, the facilitator should be able to redirect the conversation back to the manager's performance. Similarly, a facilitator can help a manager find positive ways to use the board's feedback instead of getting defensive.

? Questions for Discussion

1. Who will provide leadership during the manager's evaluation process? The board chair or mayor? A subcommittee of the board?
2. Will an internal person conduct the evaluation, will an external facilitator be hired, or will a partial in-house/consultant method be used?
3. What will be the responsibilities for the parties involved? Who will decide on the evaluation instrument? Who will facilitate the evaluation conversation? Who will gather feedback and prepare a summary report?

When Should the Manager's Performance Evaluation Take Place?

There are a variety of options for when to do performance evaluations. If the organization routinely does annual reviews on employees' anniversary dates, conducting the review on the manager's hire date is consistent with how other reviews are done and may reduce confusion for the manager and other personnel responsible for coordinating and documenting the review. Using hire dates for performance evaluations also allows the organization to stagger reviews and avoid having all employee reviews due at once.

Another advantage of using the manager's hire date for the annual performance evaluation is that it gives the manager a full year of employment to complete the tasks initially assigned. If the performance evaluation is scheduled at a time other than the hire date, the manager's first review may occur soon after hiring—or it may be postponed for over a year, leaving a new manager without formal feedback for a long time and possibly leading to false assumptions on the part of the manager or the board. For example, if the manager has not received any negative feedback through the year, the manager might assume that board members are generally pleased, while board members might think that the manager has assumed too much authority and is operating independently of the board. A lack of clear expectations and regular feedback can quickly devolve into a situation where good people with good intentions simply misunderstand each other. Consistent communication is imperative for the manager-board relationship to work successfully, and the annual evaluation process is a key component of that communication.

Scheduling the evaluation for the manager's hire date can be a problem, however, if the timing is inconsistent with the annual work schedule for the board. A midyear hire date, for instance, may mean that the board and manager are balancing budget negotiations and the annual evaluation, and it can be difficult to incorporate the governing board's annual priorities into the manager's work plan. Consider the example of a governing board that holds an annual planning retreat in February each year and hires a new manager in September. At the retreat, the board members discuss their goals for the community and identify priorities for the coming year. The manager has a set of priority tasks to complete during the first year. At the February retreat, however, the manager learns that the board is interested in accomplishing several goals that were not on the list of tasks given to the manager in September. The manager must then determine whether the tasks in the work plan are still the board's priority or if the goals set at the retreat are the ones to pursue. This situation becomes especially challenging if the manager's performance review in September was positive and then a new board majority was elected in November. The new majority may have very different goals from the previous governing board and may adopt new priorities at the winter retreat. If the manager does not seek additional clarification about how the new governing board's priorities affect the manager's responsibilities, the performance expectations of the manager and board may diverge.

A second option is to schedule the manager's evaluation around the time the board has a regular planning retreat in the winter. If the manager's evaluation is completed in advance of the retreat, accomplishments can be documented and ongoing work identified prior to planning for the next year. A benefit of conducting evaluations in the late fall or early winter is that the governing board can get an in-depth update on work accomplished since the last strategic planning session and identify priorities that still need attention. Another advantage is that this is typically a slower time of the year, and the manager and board members can take time to be reflective. The budget is in place, any new members of the governing board have been sworn in, and the manager has had enough time to complete major projects.

A disadvantage of linking the manager's performance review to the board's strategic planning cycle, however, is that the board may become focused on the manager's work plan rather than on the board's priorities for the future of the community. If the board begins to look at the manager's performance evaluation as the only way to benchmark its own accomplishments, there is a danger of the manager's work plan becoming the board's strategic plan. Of course, the manager is responsible for implementing the board's policy priorities in a given year—but the board's priorities should be more ambitious and comprehensive than the manager's work plan. If the manager's performance evaluation is used as the major source of feedback on the board's strategic plan, the board misses the opportunity to assess its own progress and reflect on what it has or has not done to accomplish its own goals.

A third option is to conduct the manager's evaluation in advance of approving the budget. This enables the board to decide whether or not to include a raise for the manager in the annual budget. If the manager accomplished the goals on the work plan, the governing board may use these accomplishments to justify a raise. Similarly, if the manager failed to complete agreed-upon goals, the governing board has a justifiable reason not to give the manager raise. The latter example could also provide the board with a legitimate reason to let a poorly performing manager go.

Another benefit of tying the manager's performance evaluation to the budget cycle is that it allows the board to allocate resources accordingly. If the local governing board is operating with a tight budget, members are unlikely to support putting additional money in the manager's salary line to cover a prospective positive evaluation. Conducting the performance evaluation before the budget is approved prevents the board from having to estimate how much money is needed for the manager's salary.

The downside of linking the budget cycle and the performance evaluation is that the conversation may be influenced by monetary incentives. Performance evaluation has an inherent value apart from financial reward, and linking the two often diminishes the focus on the intrinsic value of the manager's work. Most public servants have chosen their work because they care about their communities, not because they think they are going to make a lot of money. If the public manager's evaluation is conducted in conjunction with the budget cycle, the governing board and the public may begin to think that the only reason the manager is undergoing an evaluation is to get a raise. Disentangling the evaluation from the budgeting process can reduce the perception that the evaluation is primarily designed to decide levels of compensation.

In summary, there is no single answer to the question of when the manager's performance should take place. Each local government should consider the pros and cons discussed above and make a decision based on its own unique circumstances.

Where Should the Evaluation Discussion Take Place?

The location selected for the performance evaluation can influence its outcome. Although it may be convenient to conduct the manager's evaluation in the regular council chamber (or another room regularly used for closed sessions), these environments are associated with formal activities and may create unintended tension, especially if members of the board are all on one side of the table and the manager is on the other side. Even when people sit around a table, they are likely to sit in their regular seats, thus reinforcing formal roles and relationships.

As a best practice, individuals participating in the evaluation should gather in a neutral space, thereby reducing the chance that people will sit in their customary seats and play traditional roles.[5] Most local governments have conference rooms or can gain access to other public meeting spaces nearby. The board chair or mayor should try to encourage having people sit in a configuration other than their usual board-meeting arrangement. If possible, people should sit around the room or around a table facing one another. The manager should be seated in the same way that the members of the governing board are in order to emphasize the fact that the manager, too, has an important voice in the performance evaluation.

---

5. Brian Gunia and Brice Corgnet, "Did I Do That? Group Positioning and Asymmetry in Attributional Bias," *IACM 23rd Annual Conference Paper*, May 20, 2010, https://dx.doi.org/10.2139/ssrn.1612508. Also see Westside Toastmasters, "Maximize the Impact of Seating Formations," chap. 17 in *Dimensions of Body Language*, accessed October 13, 2025, http://westsidetoastmasters.com/resources/book_of_body_language/chap17.html.

How Long Should the Evaluation Discussion Last?

Performance evaluation is an important event for a manager, and even though board members may not have the same level of interest, they should still make every attempt to provide the manager with worthwhile feedback. To allow sufficient time for feedback and discussion, the governing board and manager should plan on the session lasting at least two hours. In some instances, they may not need all of the time, but it is better to be prepared for in-depth conversation and have the time available than to find that people have to leave before the discussion can be completed.

Ideally, a governing board and manager will set aside time for a stand-alone session expressly for performance evaluation rather than tack it onto the end of a regular board meeting. If at all possible, it is advisable that the governing board avoid doing the evaluation at the end of a regular meeting, when members of the board and the manager are tired and ready to go home. If governing-board meetings are held in the evenings, people will have worked a full day and then attended a board meeting, and it may be difficult for them to give the manager's evaluation their full attention. They may also be tempted to rush through the process.

A stand-alone session for performance evaluation still needs to be announced as a public meeting of the board, but once the governing board convenes, it immediately goes into closed session for the purpose of discussing personnel. In this way, the public is aware that the governing board and manager are taking time to discuss performance, but the conversation itself is protected from public view.

? Questions for Discussion

1. When and how often will the manager's performance evaluation take place? What is the rationale for doing the performance evaluation at a specific time?
2. Has sufficient time been set aside for the performance review? Is the time convenient for all participants?
3. Will the selected location be conducive to a productive conversation? Can seating be arranged so that everyone can see each other?

What Are the Major Steps in a Performance Evaluation?

A good performance evaluation is one where the governing board and manager agree on all the steps in the process. Table 2 provides an overview of the key steps in a performance evaluation: planning, selecting or developing an instrument, gathering data, preparing a summary report, conducting the performance review, and following up. Each of these steps is discussed in more detail in the following sections.

Planning

The first step is for the governing board and the manager to plan the performance evaluation. When a performance evaluation comes as a surprise to the members of the governing board, there is a good chance that some of the individuals who need to participate will be unavailable. Furthermore, if the evaluation process does not have support from everyone involved, there may be resentment and a lack of commitment to it. The planning process should begin a full year before the assessment instrument is used by the board to evaluate the manager. It is advisable to reach agreement on the following relatively straightforward issues early on:

- When will the evaluation take place?
- Where will the evaluation be held?
- Who will participate in the evaluation process?

Instrument Design

Once the manager and board have agreed on when the evaluation will be conducted and by whom, the next step is to design the performance-evaluation instrument. The following issues need to be decided:

- Will the governing board and manager modify another performance-evaluation instrument to fit their specific needs?
- Will the governing board create a performance-evaluation instrument by using the manager's job description or annual work plan as the basis for review?

If another instrument is used as a starting point, the board and manager should agree on what items are or are not appropriate for the manager's review. For example, it may be tempting to start with the evaluation tool used to assess department heads within the organization. However, the level of expertise and breadth of oversight that the governing board expects of the manager typically will not be reflected in an instrument for

Table 2. Steps and Activities for Effective Performance Evaluations

Step	Description	Major Activities
Planning	Determine when and where the evaluation will occur and who will participate.	• Agree on who will participate. • Decide date and time.[a] • Reserve location.
Instrument design	Decide what to evaluate and how performance will be rated.	• Select measures for evaluation (5–7 critical areas). • Determine scale and clearly define what each rating means. • Decide means of distribution. • Assign responsibility for data collection and compilation of summary ratings.
Data collection	Decide how and by whom information will be collected.	• Distribute assessment as hard and/or electronic copy. • Provide firm deadline. • Follow up with nonresponders before deadline. • Prepare data sheet of individual results.
Summary report	Prepare a written overview of the assessment responses.	• Determine number of responses for each question. • Compute an average board rating for each item. • Determine range of board ratings for each item. • Prepare summary report showing board average, range, and manager rating (if applicable). • Compile written feedback.
Performance review	Facilitate conversation regarding manager's performance among members of the board and manager.	• Agree on ground rules for the performance review. • Review the rating scale. • Discuss evaluation items.[b]
Follow-up	Identify areas for improvement and propose performance-improvement objectives for the coming cycle.	• Do a gap analysis. • Develop a performance plan for developmental goals. • Create goals and performance expectations for the upcoming cycle.

[a] Ensure that sufficient time is set aside for the evaluation conversation.

[b] This discussion should focus on how to improve performance and/or reduce differences in perceptions. Participants should provide specific examples of problems and suggest actions that would be more effective.

department heads. Department heads usually are responsible for a set of specific functions within their units, while a manager is usually expected to provide direction and oversight for the entire organization. The evaluation instrument for the manager should focus on expected outcomes for the organization and not on the particular manner in which the manager conforms to organizational rules. If specific performance problems are a concern for the governing board, it is best to address them as they happen rather than wait for the manager's formal evaluation.

The ICMA's website provides an example of specific performance items and instrument formats that managers and boards may borrow or adapt to meet their needs.[6] Elected officials can also contact the School of Government for opportunities to take a course in manager and board evaluations and to obtain other sample evaluation instruments. It is important to remember, however, that a good performance evaluation always reflects the unique requirements of a particular manager serving a particular board. An instrument from another organization is unlikely to match all of those requirements.

The board and manager need to agree on the rating scale to be used in the evaluation process. (See page 29 for examples.) A common set of performance ratings is "below expectations," "meets expectations," and "exceeds expectations." (This approach assumes that the governing board and manager have established clear expectations prior to implementing the performance evaluation). Another common scale for performance reviews is a Likert Scale, where numbers from one to four or one to five are used to indicate a range from "strongly disagree" (the lowest number) to "strongly agree" (the highest number). If an even-numbered scale is used, raters will be forced to indicate whether they agree or disagree because there is no midpoint for a neutral rating. An odd-numbered scale allows raters to be undecided or neutral on a given question (for example, by choosing three on a scale from one to five). A performance evaluation that comes back with a lot of undecided or neutral responses offers little guidance on how to improve performance. For that reason, it may be best to design an instrument that allows for more communication between the board and the manager.

---

6. These performance appraisals can be found on the association's website at https://icma.org/documents/sample-appraisal-performance.

Sample Performance Measure and Rating Scales

Read the performance measure "Budgeting and Financial Management" below and then review the different rating scales. What are the advantages and disadvantages of the different scales?

Budgeting and financial management: Preparing and administering the budget as well as interpreting financial information to assess the short-term and long-term fiscal condition of the community, determining the cost-effectiveness of programs, and comparing alternative strategies.

Sample 3-Point Scale

☐ Needs improvement   ☐ Meets expectations   ☐ Exceeds expectations

Note: This rating scale would translate into "1, 2, 3" for purposes of a summary rating.

Sample 4-Point Scale

1 = Never   2 = Sometimes   3 = Often   4 = Always   X = Unable to rate

Note: This scale has no midpoint or "neutral" option, forcing people to express an opinion.

Sample 5-Point Scale

```
-----------1---------------2---------------3---------------4---------------5---------------X---------
```
Does not meet expectations   Meets expectations   Exceeds expectations   Unable to rate

Note: Any items scored *unable to rate* should be left out of the board's summary rating. If a majority of board members cannot rate the item, then no average should be created and the item should be dropped from the summary.

Sample 10-Point Scale

Rate from 1–10, 10 being excellent   1   2   3   4   5   6   7   8   9   10

Note: A 10-point scale gives raters more flexibility but may not lead to clearer results. What would be the difference, for instance, between an average rating of 7.25 and an average rating of 7.75?

Sample Anchored Scale

Fails to use controls to influence efficiency or cost-effectiveness. Consistently shows significant budget variances without acceptable justifications. Often wastes resources by not carefully reviewing impact of decisions. Fails to follow up when resources are not properly utilized.	Ineffective
	Moderately effective
Utilizes available controls and procedures to monitor resource use effectively and devises appropriate and timely corrective actions as necessary. Efficiently uses resources by evaluating alternatives, selecting appropriate strategies, and implementing best allocation of resources. Budget variances are within acceptable limits.	Effective
Develops and implements innovative methods to enhance effectiveness in planning, monitoring, and controlling resources. Aggressively seeks out methods to enhance efficiency and cost reduction. Implements innovative and productive means to stretch and supplement resources while enhancing operations and services. Incorporates comprehensive analyses of financial impact in decision-making process.	Highly effective
	Exceptionally effective

Note: An anchored scale uses the same rating system for each item, but the statements describing what each rating means will link to the item being rated. This is the most sophisticated system and ensures that every person's rating is based on a shared understanding of what the score means. However, developing an anchored scale can be costly and time-consuming.

Another design choice is whether the instrument will be available online or administered in hard copy. An online survey is easier to administer and maintains confidentiality for respondents. Another advantage of an online tool is that individual responses are recorded directly into the system, which eliminates the potential for human error in entering the responses. Most online tools provide space for people to add open-ended comments in addition to the numeric ratings. There are a number of online-survey services that can be used to create a tool that every member of the governing board and the manager can use.

If members of the governing board are uncomfortable using an electronic survey, the HR director or facilitator can distribute hard copies of the instrument to every member of the governing board. If hard copies are used, extreme care should be taken to ensure that the raw feedback is given only to the person designated to summarize the individual responses. Confidentiality for members of the governing board is harder to guarantee with a hard-copy survey. Clear instructions need to be included so that board members and the manager understand how the instruments will be collected and summarized.

Data Collection

Everyone participating in the performance evaluation should clearly understand how to complete the instrument, what will be done to ensure confidentiality, and who will compile results. If individuals are unclear about how to complete the instrument, they are likely to submit an incomplete or inaccurate review. For example, if the instrument asks people to rate performance using a five-point Likert Scale, but the scale is not clearly labeled, some people may think that the highest rating is one while others may think it is five. A well-designed evaluation instrument will include both written and verbal instructions.

Everyone participating in the evaluation should also have sufficient time to complete the form. There is no fixed rule for how much time to allow. The board members and manager need enough time to be thoughtful in completing the evaluation, but if too much lead time is provided, the task may be set aside for more pressing priorities and people may forget to complete it. Usually, a two-week window is long enough for people to find time to complete the evaluation, but not so long that it is forgotten.

Average Rating and Range

The *average rating* for each item is computed by dividing the sum of the board members' ratings by the number of responses for that question (for example, if four members of a five-member board gave the manager a total rating of 15 points, the average score would be 15 divided by 4, or 3.75). The *range* is simply the lowest and highest of the board ratings for each item (for example, if an item were rated by two board members as a 1, by one board member as a 2, and by another board member as a 3, the range would be 1:3).

Summary Report

Once the evaluation forms have been completed, a summary report must be prepared. The summary should include, at a minimum, the following information:

- the actual number of responses for each question,
- the average board rating for each question, and
- the range of board ratings for each item.

(See the box above.)

If the evaluation tool offers a space for raters to make written comments on each item or an overall comment at the end, the comments can be incorporated into the numeric report for each item or provided as an attachment to the summary report.

For an evaluation to be considered and a summary report prepared, a majority of board members should have completed the instrument. Ideally, every member of the governing board will take the time to complete it. Sometimes, one member will not complete the evaluation form because of time constraints or because that member is satisfied with the manager's performance and does not believe that it is important to communicate with the manager through the instrument. Although it is best to have everyone's input, the manager works for the governing board as a whole, and if a majority of board members have completed the performance evaluation, it is better to move forward than to hold up the process. If a majority of board members fail to complete the evaluation, the mayor or board chair should revisit how to proceed.

When summarizing the results, it is important to indicate the number of people who responded to each item. Ratings by individual members of the board, however, should not appear in the report. The summary evaluation should reflect only a single score for the board. During the meeting to review the manager's performance, individuals are free to offer verbal examples and give praise or criticism, but the summary evaluation should reflect the board's average ratings and the majority recommendations. Note, however, that both the individual members' responses and the summary should be placed in the manager's personnel file.[7]

The amount of time needed to prepare the summary report will vary depending upon the nature of the performance evaluation and the manner in which it was presented. The report for an online evaluation can usually be prepared quickly because the data have already been entered and need only be consolidated and formatted. If the evaluation was done on paper, the person summarizing the results will have to type each response into a single document, which can be time-consuming.

If the manager has completed a self-evaluation, it may be provided as a separate document or it may be included with the summary of board-member responses. The manager and board need to use the same assessment instrument. In a combined report, the results should be presented in such a way that everyone can easily see where the manager and board agree and which areas need additional attention.

Evaluation Discussion

Once the summary report has been prepared, the board must schedule a session to discuss the manager's evaluation. It is helpful to set ground rules for this discussion so that the manager and board members agree on how they will conduct themselves. The board may wish to follow the sample ground rules for effective groups on page 34.

The discussion should focus on important issues, and it will be more productive if people provide specific, constructive feedback. This includes giving examples of what went wrong and why it was a problem and offering suggestions for what might work better or be more effective.

Usually, the board and manager will agree that the manager's performance is good in certain areas and needs improvement in others. It is important to acknowledge outstanding performance, but if the conversation focuses only on those things that are going well, the manager and board may miss an opportunity to identify performance problems and ways to improve. The conversation needs to include time for discussion

---

7. G.S. 160A-168(a).

Figure 3. High-Low Combinations of Manager and Board Performance Ratings

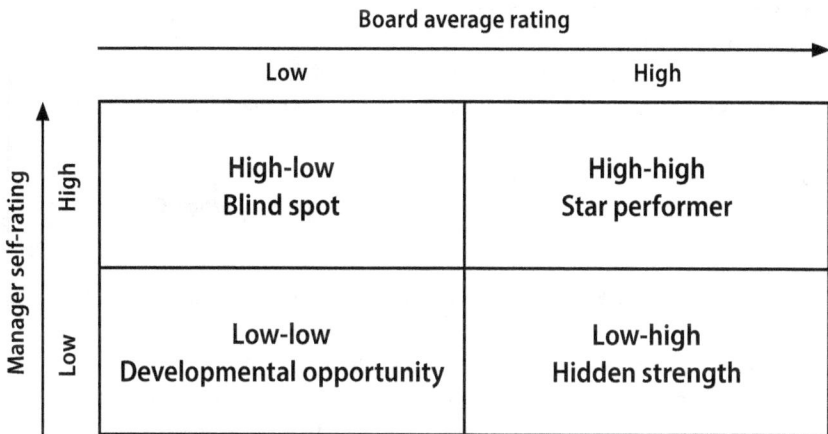

		Board average rating	
		Low	High
Manager self-rating	High	**High-low** **Blind spot**	**High-high** **Star performer**
	Low	**Low-low** **Developmental opportunity**	**Low-high** **Hidden strength**

of areas where both the board and the manager agreed there were performance concerns and areas where the manager's perception was high and the board's average perception was low. Figure 3 illustrates feedback opportunities that can result from different ratings by the board and the manager.

The discussion can be structured in a variety of ways. For those local governments using a facilitator, the facilitator will often provide guidance about the process. In some instances, members of the governing board meet beforehand to review their combined ratings of the manager, clarify what feedback they want to provide, and decide who will provide it. In other cases, the board members and manager meet collectively, with members of the board providing individual feedback to the manager in turn. Regardless of the exact approach, the feedback from the board to the manager needs to balance input from individual members with input from the board as a whole. If board members have met beforehand, they will have had a chance to air their individual concerns before discussing an agreed-upon common set of issues with the manager. This approach allows the board to give the manager comprehensive feedback. If, instead, the manager receives feedback directly from each member of the governing

Sample Ground Rules for Effective Groups (with Illustrative Examples)

Test hidden assumptions and intentions.

I'm thinking you are concerned about _____. Is this right?

What I understood was _____. What did you understand?

My interest was _____. I did not intend to make things more difficult. Can you tell me what I've done or said that I may not be aware of?

Share important information.

When you say _____, it sounds as if you may have more information. Can you share what you've heard?

What relevant information are we missing?

Let's not get bogged down in the details. What do you see as the strategic benefits or costs associated with _____?

Ensure that everyone participates, no one dominates.

We haven't heard what you think about this issue. Do you have something to add?

You have made that point clearly. What do others have to say about this?

I'm guessing your experience was different from mine. What can you tell us about how you and your community have been affected?

Use specific examples and agree on what important words mean.

Can you give me an example of how this situation has directly affected you?

Can you help me understand from your perspective how this would work?

Can you walk us through your thinking on this?

Explain your reasoning and intent.

Can you help me understand how you reached that conclusion? I'm not following your reasoning.

I'd like to share the things I thought were important for this decision. Can you give me feedback on my thought process?

We have a commitment to transparency, right? Can you help me understand why and how this decision was made and how it is in keeping with our core values?

Focus on interests, not positions.

What do you need and how does this approach meet your goals?

What concerns do you have that will not be addressed by this approach?

What would a successful resolution of this issue look like to you?

Advocate for your ideas and be curious about those of others.

It seems as though you have a preference on this issue. Can you explain what you want to do and why?

I think we should _____. What do you think?

What I saw was _____. Did I miss something?

Show appreciation for others' points of view.

Can you help me understand how you see things?

Of all the things we have discussed, what do you see as most important?

You have a lot of history in this community. What do you think people will say about this?

(continued on next page)

(continued from previous page)

Jointly design next steps and individual freedom to choose.

Let me offer a possible approach to _____. What do you think of this?

It seems to me we need to take the next step. What options do you think we have?

What issues do we need to decide as a group, and what can individuals decide on their own?

Discuss difficult issues.

I realize others want to make a decision quickly, but I'm not sure we have heard from everyone who will be affected. I don't want to put anyone on the spot, but I want to make sure our decision reflects everyone's interest. How do others feel about our asking more questions before we make a final decision?

I get the feeling people may be reluctant to make a decision right now. It is a high-risk situation, but failing to act also has consequences. Before we make a decision, can we take a moment to talk about what we are afraid might happen?

Use a decision-making approach that allows for informed decisions and generates commitment.

This is a decision I want us to be in agreement about. Can we test to see if we have consensus and commitment before moving forward? If we are not in agreement, we will need to have a special meeting to work out differences before the next regular meeting. What do others think about this approach?

This is a big issue and we will need to have strong support for it to succeed. Before calling for a vote, can we check to see if everyone is prepared to act? If people are not yet ready to decide, can we make a list of questions or concerns we need to address before taking the next step?

We need to take a long-term view and honestly assess our positives and negatives. How will we know if our current approaches are / are not working?

Find merit in others' points of view.

Even though I disagree with your conclusion, I see the value in your point of view.

I think it makes sense that you don't want to be excluded from the negotiation.

I appreciate what you have done to make this work.

Be fair and consistent in making decisions, no matter who is affected.

We are committed to hearing from all parties affected by our decisions. Have we done that in this case?

My understanding is that we have a local policy to provide guidance in situations like this. Why are we making an exception in this case?

Historically, we have given everyone the same opportunity to _____. Can you help me understand why our approach won't work for this person or group?

Sources: Roger Fisher and Daniel Shapiro, *Beyond Reason: Using Emotions as You Negotiate* (Penguin, 2005); Roger Schwarz et al., *The Skilled Facilitator Fieldbook: Tips, Tools, and Tested Methods for Consultants, Facilitators, Managers, Trainers, and Coaches* (Jossey-Bass, 2005); "An Effective Council (Operating Principles)," UNC School of Government, accessed October 14, 2025, https://www.sog.unc.edu/sites/default/files/reports/An%20Effective%20Council.pdf.

board, care should be taken to ensure that any future actions on the part of the manager are endorsed by the majority of the board and not based on individual feedback from the evaluation session.

It is important to remember that listening is a vital aspect of an effective performance review. Not only does the manager need to listen carefully to the board members' feedback, but the members also need to allow time to listen to the manager in order to understand why some expectations may not have been met. Most professional managers will do their best to accomplish goals, but factors outside the manager's control can impede or derail progress toward stated objectives. Funding cuts, new regulations, unexpected crises, changes in board priorities, and employee turnover, for example, can interfere with a manager's overall work plan. Unless the manager and board revised the manager's annual work plan during the year to accommodate unexpected changes, the manager's evaluation may end up being based on goals that were, in fact, unachievable. If this is the case, the evaluation instrument and process will need to be redesigned to adapt to new realities.

It is also important for the board and manager to remain focused on the areas being evaluated. If members of the governing board or the manager bring up issues that are unrelated to the specific objectives for the performance review, the manager or the board members themselves may be caught off guard. What if one of the objectives was for the manager to develop a capital-improvement plan and, during the evaluation, a board member criticizes the manager for failing to establish a contract for building a new water-treatment plant? If the board's expectation was for the manager to have a *plan* for capital improvement—not to *contract* for specific projects—the board member's criticism is not relevant to the manager's evaluation.

Finally, board members should keep in mind that people respond better to praise than to criticism. The performance review and subsequent follow-up will be more productive if board members provide feedback on how the manager can be more successful rather than emphasizing things that went wrong.

Follow-Up

After the evaluation, the board and manager need to ask the following questions:

- What are the subsequent steps for the manager after the performance evaluation? Next steps may include determining compensation or bonuses and establishing goals for the next year.
- What steps will the manager and the board take to ensure that issues will be addressed?
- How will the board and the manager evaluate progress along the way?

? Questions for Discussion

It may be helpful to do a gap analysis of the goals for the manager's performance and how well the manager achieved those goals. The board should ask the following questions:

1. If few goals were met, was it because the goals were too high to begin with?
2. Were goals not met due to circumstances outside the manager's control?
3. Were goals not met because members of the board kept changing their expectations during the year?
4. If goals were exceeded, were the goals not set high enough?
5. Did the manager really go above and beyond the call of duty?
6. Should the board set more ambitious goals for the next cycle?

Board Evaluation

People with power are expected to assume responsibility as a part of their authority, and public officials are expected to be answerable to the elected legislature or the electorate. It is unrealistic for the public to hold local elected officials accountable for every action of a local government, but it is reasonable to expect a governing board to set and monitor goals for the organization and themselves.[1] The governing board is ultimately accountable for organizational activity and accomplishment.[2] To fulfill their accountability role, elected officials need to understand what they are accountable for, recognize how their performance affects other parts of the organization, and identify ways to obtain feedback and improve their oversight role.

Conscientious elected officials want to do a good job for their community and their local government, and they want to know that they are representing themselves and their community well. Governing-board members "must take it upon themselves to look critically at their individual and collective roles and seek to make constructive changes."[3] The following sections focus on assessing the governing board's performance.

---

1. Carolyn Oliver, "Board Accountability in Highly Constrained Environments," *Board Leadership* 2005, no. 80 (2005): 2–5.

2. John Carver, *Boards That Make a Difference: A New Design for Leadership in Nonprofit and Public Organizations* (Jossey-Bass, 1997), 2. Also see J. E. Pynes, *Human Resources Management for Public and Nonprofit Organizations* (Jossey-Bass, 1997).

3. James H. Svara, "Contributions of the City Council to Effective Governance," *Popular Government* 51, no. 4 (1986): 5.

What Is the Standard for Board Accountability?

There is no single standard for board accountability. Municipal and county elected officials are held accountable for different things in different ways. For instance, municipal councils and boards of county commissioners are responsible for (1) following local, state, and federal laws; (2) working with others on the board, in government, and in the community; (3) setting direction and making policy; (4) overseeing local government finances; and (5) making sure the local government is accountable. Board members also are required to adopt and abide by a code of ethics.[4] Exactly what specific local elected officials are responsible for in each of these areas differs, as do the penalties for failure. Board members should annually agree upon what the local board is responsible for in each of these areas, what performance standards they will use to accomplish shared work, and how they will hold themselves accountable for meeting these expectations.

At a minimum, a public governing board's goals should include at least one item in each of the following areas:

- operating within the board's legal authority and carrying out both policymaking and adjudicatory duties with obedience, care, and loyalty;
- building effective teams by working well as a board and with the local government manager and other professional staff;
- engaging members of the public and organizational partners in fulfilling the organization's mission and purpose;
- planning strategically for the community's future by determining what programs and services will be provided to whom and at what level of quality;
- ensuring that resources are adequate and effectively managed to provide services; and
- supporting the manager and reviewing the manager's and the board's performance in order to provide oversight for resources, programs, and services.[5]

---

4. G.S. 160A-86. Also see A. Fleming Bell, II, *A Model Code of Ethics for North Carolina Local Elected Officials* (School of Government, 2010).

5. Richard T. Ingram, *Ten Basic Responsibilities of Nonprofit Boards* (National Center for Nonprofit Boards, 2008). Also see Vaughn Mamlin Upshaw, "Essential Responsibilities of Local Governing Boards," *Popular Government* 71, no. 2 (2006): 14–25.

? Questions for Discussion

1. What does accountability mean for me in my present role?
2. What do I hold the board, manager, and organization accountable for?
3. What do I know now about accountability that I wish I had known when I was newly elected?
4. What can be done to make our governing board, manager, or organization more accountable?

Why Should the Board Evaluate Itself?

There is growing evidence that organizational effectiveness is associated with governing boards that perform effectively.[6] While most of the research on board effectiveness has been done in corporate and nonprofit arenas, many of these lessons are relevant to public governing boards and managers. Private, public, and nonprofit governing boards are all responsible for things such as overseeing resources, selecting and evaluating the chief executive or manager, monitoring programs and services, and providing strategic direction for their organizations. Research on effective governance indicates that boards involved in setting strategy for their organizations and boards with members who work well interpersonally create more value for their organizations than boards that do not perform well in these areas.[7] Elected officials committed to good government will benefit

6. Robert D. Herman and David O. Renz, "Board Practices of Especially Effective and Less Effective Local Nonprofit Organizations," *American Review of Public Administration* 30, no. 2 (June 2000): 146–60. The survey instrument measured mission definition and review, CEO selection and review, working relationship between board and CEO, program selection consistent with mission and program monitoring, giving and soliciting contributions, financial management, strategic planning, new board-member selection and training, working relationships between board and staff, marketing and public relations, conduct of board and committee meetings, and role in risk management.

7. Coral B. Ingley and Nicholas T. Van der Walt, "The Strategic Board: The Changing Role of Directors in Developing and Maintaining Corporate Capability," *Corporate Governance* 9, no. 3 (2001): 174–85.

from board evaluation because it enables them to improve the effectiveness, efficiency, and accountability of the governing board and the local government.

Scenario for Discussion

After a hard-fought campaign for city council, a new member walks into the city hall excited about attending her first meeting as a member of the board. As she approaches the meeting room, she stops to listen to a conversation between two members just inside the doorway. "What are we going to do?" one person says. "There is no way she's going to support our proposal to cut funding for public works." The other person responds, "She doesn't have to know we are proposing a cut. As far as she knows, funding is going to be at the same level as it was last year. What she doesn't know won't hurt her."

Taking a deep breath, the new member steps into the room and nods at the two men standing nearby. The men quickly look away, take their seats, and start shuffling papers. Looking over the agenda for the meeting, the new member sees an item on the consent agenda to change the schedule for sidewalk improvements. She considers what she overheard and wonders if the public works budget will be cut if the sidewalk project is postponed. She knows that some of the neighborhoods in her district have been waiting for years for the city to put in sidewalks. "I can't allow this to be put off," she thinks to herself.

The mayor calls the meeting to order. There is a quick motion and vote to approve the agenda and another to approve the minutes from the previous meeting. The mayor then asks for a motion to approve the consent agenda. The new member proposes moving the item on rescheduling sidewalks from the consent agenda to the regular agenda. The two men she overheard talking before the meeting look at each other and roll their eyes. "Here we go," one murmurs. The other replies, "I told you she was going to cause trouble for us."

The new member considers her situation. "What have I done wrong?" she asks herself. "I wish I had a better sense of the unwritten rules and knew more about how to get things

accomplished without alienating others." Scribbling on a
notepad, she soon has a long list of questions about how to
work with the other members of the council and how to move
her issues forward. As she looks at her list, she realizes that
she has no clue about where to find answers to her questions.
"After the meeting, I'll ask the mayor," she decides.

? Scenario Questions

- How has communication broken down in this situation?
- How could a board orientation been used to avoid this situation and others like it?
- How can boards develop their own processes for dealing with communication and policy discussions?

What Should Board Members Consider Before Implementing an Evaluation?

Evaluation can be challenging for any governing board. Evaluation for local government boards in North Carolina is particularly challenging because public boards are bound by open-meeting laws and "a discussion of a board's relationship within itself—that is, how the members work together and how they might improve"—must take place in an open session.[8] Members of the board should understand that a board evaluation process presents both benefits and challenges for the governing body. Before initiating an evaluation, board members should weigh the pros and cons of the evaluation process and decide if they are prepared to proceed. Table 3 presents a list of benefits and challenges generated by local government elected officials attending a program at the School of Government.[9]

---

8. David M. Lawrence, *Open Meetings and Local Governments in North Carolina*, 7th ed. (School of Government, 2008), 27.

9. Results of group discussion during Manager Evaluation and Board Accountability Workshop, School of Government, April 2007.

Table 3. Perceived Pros and Cons of Board Assessment

Pros	Cons
Establishes a common language and shared understanding of what it means to work well as a governing body.	Sheds light on potential problems within the board; opens board up to negative feedback and fear because "people don't like to look in the mirror."
Serves as a tool for focusing discussions on how to improve the governing body's work. Identifies it in order to improve it.	Takes time to design, implement, review, and decide what action to take based on the evaluation results.
Provides a way for governing body to reflect on how well its actions matched its agreements.	Provides little recourse for governing body as a whole if individual members do not abide by agreed-upon norms.
Focuses the governing body's attention on actions that contribute to the local government's mission and goals for the community. Improves services to the community.	Puts pressure on board members to respond if governance problems are identified. Members who say they support change may risk seeming disingenuous if they do not then follow through.
Provides direct feedback from citizens.	Can convey the impression that the board lacks an understanding of the public.

Although members may be uncomfortable publicly discussing poor board performance, it is generally no secret when a public governing body is ineffective or even dysfunctional. Intractable governing problems usually extend beyond the actions of any individual member or any particular composition of members on the governing board. Ineffective relationships and mistrust often become ingrained in the culture and ongoing practices, making it difficult for one person or even a group of board members to alter the performance of the board.[10] By engaging in an evaluation of its work, however, a governing board may identify areas of strength and reaffirm members' commitment to making a difference for the local government and community.

---

10. Roger Fisher and Scott Brown, *Getting Together: Building a Relationship That Gets to Yes* (Houghton Mifflin, 1988), 129.

What Constitutes an Effective Board Evaluation?

Board evaluations are most effective when they reflect members' perceptions of how they are currently doing and how they would like to perform in the future. They are a process for learning about individual perceptions and communicating the individual perceptions to the group.[11] It is important for the evaluation to focus on how the board operates as a whole, not on the performance or behaviors of individual members. The goal is to develop the board's ability to discuss its shared work and come up with ideas about how to move forward on common goals.

Do All Board Evaluations Look Alike?

The process and instrument used for a board evaluation will vary depending upon the board's purposes. Any board evaluation needs to assist the governing board in accomplishing its goals, but one board's goals may be quite different from another's. Using an instrument that covers everything the board is responsible for can result in feedback that is too diffuse. A good evaluation asks about issues that are important for effective board performance and those that are related to a board's annual goals.

Topics for board evaluation often include the following:

- board member roles and responsibilities,
- working relationships between board members and professional staff,
- public engagement,
- community partnerships,
- long-term capital investments, and
- oversight and monitoring of organizational performance.

Appendix B provides a list of sample board-evaluation items.

A board can seek feedback on its performance in a variety of ways. For instance, at the end of each meeting, the board chair or mayor can quickly go around and ask members for feedback about what went well and what could be improved. This type of feedback is useful for specific issues related to how the board operates as a body, but it is likely to focus on incremental

---

11. Diane J. Duca, *Nonprofit Boards: Roles, Responsibilities and Performance* (John Wiley and Sons, Inc., 1996).

changes needed to improve meeting management rather than on long-term goals. In a more traditional evaluation, members assess the effectiveness of their board's actions, expectations, and priorities. Even if the evaluation is limited to a few key topics, the assessment will give members an opportunity to discuss issues important to the board's performance.

Which Evaluation Instrument Should Be Used?

Evaluations are highly subjective and unique to particular organizations. It is unusual for a board to find a ready-made tool that is perfectly suited to its needs. Instead, the board should identify the areas that board members want to assess and review different evaluation items and sample instruments.

In general, it is helpful to use an evaluation instrument that lets people provide two rankings for each item. For each item, members indicate where they want the board to be (perhaps on a scale of one to five) and also rate where the board currently is (using the same scale.) This allows members to see if there are differences among their expectations for the board and to identify differences between current and expected performance. The evaluation can reveal areas of consensus and shared goals, or it can uncover differences in perception and draw attention to areas that need to be addressed. For example, if some people rate communication among board members as "poor" and others rate it as "excellent," the range of scores indicates a difference in members' perspectives and gives the board an opportunity to clarify expectations and suggest ways to improve.

If a governing board is divided or unclear about what type of feedback would be most useful, members can complete a quick-scan evaluation. A quick-scan evaluation covers a wide range of topics at a very high level. If a majority of members agree that an area needs improvement, a more in-depth set of questions can be developed to look at various aspects of board performance. A quick-scan also reveals areas where members disagree about the board's performance. If members' ratings include a wide range of responses (for example, from "strongly disagree" to "strongly agree"), that is an indication that board members do not see the issue in the same way and would benefit from further clarification about expectations for the board in this area. Appendix C presents an example of a quick-scan evaluation.

Who Should Participate in the Board's Evaluation?

Board evaluations can be enhanced with input from selected individuals and groups familiar with the responsibilities and working relationships of the board. Without such input, a board may be limited to making only modest changes, leaving major underlying problems and responsibilities unrecognized.[12] The governing board may invite participation from people who routinely observe and are affected by its work, including the manager, clerk, attorney, and department heads. It may also seek input from key external groups, such as advisory boards, business leaders, and informed citizens.

Some boards choose to use an external facilitator to help with the evaluation process. Knowledgeable facilitators can provide examples of evaluation tools, compile information, prepare a neutral report, and ensure that the feedback process is handled in a fair and respectful manner. The facilitator can also organize a retreat for elected officials to discuss the results and help identify strategies to address issues uncovered during the evaluation.

What Are the Steps in Board Evaluation?

A board's evaluation process needs to be carefully planned before being implemented. Members of the board will be frustrated if the evaluation process is poorly conducted, the evaluation tool is inconsistent with board priorities, or the process puts individual board members on the spot. A successful evaluation process is one that guides the governing board in (1) preparing, planning, and administering the evaluation; (2) discussing the evaluation results and establishing priorities; and (3) acting on the findings. Figure 4 illustrates the steps in a board-evaluation process.

An effective board-evaluation process is one in which

- board members agree on what they will evaluate;
- appropriate measures are included in the evaluation instrument;
- all board members complete an evaluation and submit it to a board chair or other designated neutral person;

---

12. Thomas P. Holland, "Self-Assessment by Nonprofit Boards," *Nonprofit Management and Leadership* 2, no. 1 (1991): 25–36.

- the neutral person compiles a single summary report including both the average rating and the range of ratings for each item;
- the board sets aside sufficient time to discuss the feedback of the evaluation (note that the results of a board evaluation must be discussed in an open meeting);
- members agree on priorities and action steps; and
- there is an opportunity for people to provide feedback on the evaluation process itself.

When and Where Should the Discussion of the Evaluation Take Place?

Before the evaluation process starts, it is important to decide when and where the results of the evaluation will be discussed. There is rarely enough time in a regularly scheduled meeting for the governing board to engage in a thoughtful discussion. The board needs to have enough time to reflect on the evaluation feedback and set goals for itself. Orientation or team-building sessions and retreats often provide such an opportunity.

What Type of Follow-Up Is Necessary?

After the board discusses the evaluation results, members should develop a set of goals for improving performance. Even if board members agree that they are doing well, there are usually opportunities for improvement. Where performance is below expectations, the discussion should focus on what the board can do differently to be more successful moving forward. A guide for an ongoing improvement process appears in Figure 5.

As a first step, the board should look at its list of goals and select a limited number of areas for improvement. Even under ideal circumstances, it is difficult for boards to improve skills in more than three to five areas at a time, and too many priorities will be overwhelming for the group. Focusing on the issues that a majority of members agree are important will be most likely to yield positive results. The board should then establish measurable and time-bound performance targets for each priority and incorporate these into the annual calendar used to monitor progress.

The next step is to develop an action plan for each priority. Regardless of the plan a board approves, little will happen if members of the board neglect

Figure 4. Board Evaluation Process

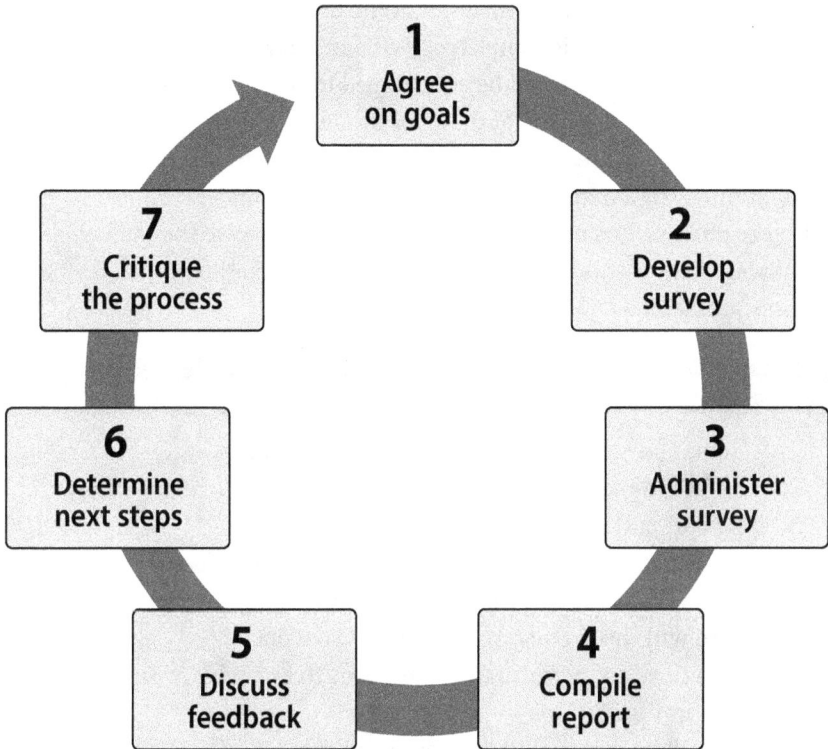

Figure 5. Process for Committing to Ongoing Improvement

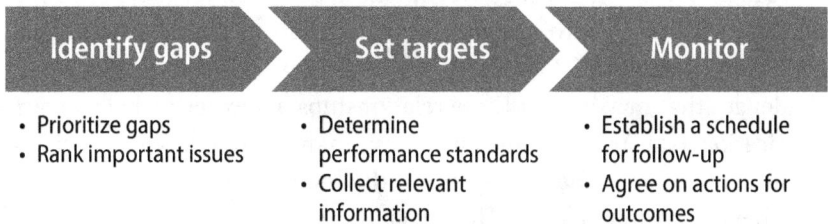

Identify gaps	Set targets	Monitor
• Prioritize gaps • Rank important issues	• Determine performance standards • Collect relevant information	• Establish a schedule for follow-up • Agree on actions for outcomes

to follow through. One way to make sure the work gets done is to appoint an individual or a subcommittee to champion each change and monitor its progress. Doing so will help ensure that the board stays on track.

After the evaluation is completed, the board may find it useful to critique the process. Members should be encouraged to suggest improvements, and the board should make note of these for use in future evaluations.

Boards should use the list of questions below to plan for the board evaluation. While managers can help by identifying a facilitator to help with the process, it is not appropriate to directly involve the manager. For example, board members should not ask the manager to opine on who or what is problematic about the board.

? Questions for Discussion

1. What is the purpose of the board's evaluation?
2. Have board members outlined what they expect of each other?
3. Who will participate in the review process?
4. Will the board use an external facilitator for the evaluation process?
5. When will the evaluation be scheduled?
6. Where will the evaluation discussion take place?
7. Who will select performance measures to be included in the evaluation tool?
8. Who will be responsible for compiling results into a single report and providing average ratings and ranges for each item?
9. How will we coordinate the board-evaluation process with the manager's performance review?
10. How will the board set measurable performance targets and be responsible for monitoring changes in performance?

A high-performing local government depends on strong, collaborative relationships—both among elected officials and between officials, management, and staff. Evaluation processes play a key role in identifying challenges that may impact these relationships. By fostering better communication, transparency, and awareness, many conflicts can be avoided. Evaluations of both the manager and the board serve as valuable tools to enhance communication. The resources included in the remainder of this Board Builder are designed to support boards in creating their own effective evaluation processes.

Appendix A.
Practices for Effective Local Government Management

The International City/County Management Association (ICMA) has identified thirteen core competencies that members believe are important to being an effective local government manager.[1]

Note: When administering and scoring this exercise, it is important to take into account the positions of the participants. Varied roles in the organization will lead to varied responses.

Instructions for Participants
1. Read through the thirteen practices below.
2. Mark whether you think the management practice is highly important (H), moderately important (M), or unimportant (L) for your local government.
3. List your six most important (H) and six least important (L) practices.

---

1. "Practices for Effective Local Government Management and Leadership," ICMA, accessed October 25, 2025, https://icma.org/page/practices-effective-local-government-management-and-leadership.

Instructions for the Board

1. Tally the top priorities for the entire board to see where there are areas of agreement and disagreement on what practices are most important for your local government.
2. Once you have identified a set of priority practices, these can be used in developing a job advertisement and questions for candidates during the interview process.

Six Most Important Practices	Six Least Important Practices

Core Competencies

1. **Personal and professional integrity.** Being fair, honest, and ethical in all personal and professional relationships and activities.
2. **Community engagement.** Ensuring and managing community involvement in local government to support good decision-making.
3. **Equity and inclusion.** Creating an environment of involvement, respect, and connection of diverse ideas, backgrounds, and talent throughout the organization and the community.
4. **Staff effectiveness.** Taking responsibility for the development, performance, and success of employees throughout the organization.
5. **Personal resiliency and development.** Demonstrating a commitment to a balanced life through ongoing self-renewal and development in order to increase personal capacity.
6. **Strategic leadership.** Defining and communicating a vision and leveraging all resources and tools to achieve it.
7. **Policy facilitation and implementation.** Engaging with elected officials and other community stakeholders to create and execute policies that achieve common goals and objectives.
8. **Community and resident service.** Discerning community needs and providing responsive, equitable services.
9. **Service delivery.** Understanding the basic principles of service delivery, using strategic decision-making and continuous improvement to serve the organization and community, and influencing the components and relationships between operational areas.
10. **Technological literacy.** Demonstrating an understanding of information technology and ensuring that it is incorporated appropriately in service delivery, information sharing, and public access.
11. **Financial management and budgeting.** Implementing long-term financial analysis and planning that integrates strategic planning and reflects a community's values and priorities; preparing and administering the budget.

12. **Human resources management and workforce engagement.**
    Ensuring that the policies and procedures of the organization
    are applied consistently and fairly and motivating and
    engaging the workforce to its highest potential.
13. **Communication and information sharing.** Effectively
    facilitating the flow of ideas, information, and understanding.

Appendix B.
Sample Board-Evaluation Items

Note: These items are drawn from sample evaluations and references on board effectiveness. When selecting items for a board evaluation, it is important to focus on priorities. Try to include *no more than thirty items* on the evaluation.

Legal and Ethical

Items focus on how members receive information and orientation as well as how they adhere to laws, ethical standards, local policies, and board procedures.

Board Orientation and Information
1. Board members receive an orientation and training on their roles and responsibilities.
2. Orientation to the local government includes information about the organization's history, culture, and traditions.
3. The board's and the organization's values are written, so that everyone knows what they are.
4. Board members understand the local government's mission and how it relates to services and programs.
5. Management and staff in this organization go out of their way to make sure all board members have access to the same information.
6. Materials pertaining to significant decisions are given to members in advance of the meetings.
7. Board members arrive prepared for meetings.
8. The board regularly discusses roles and responsibilities, and every member fully understands them.

Legal and Ethical Responsibilities

9. Board members respect the spirit as well as the intent of the law in its actions.
10. The governing body reflects a sense of public service over personal interest.
11. Board members are familiar with the powers and limitations of their status as local elected officials.
12. Board members understand their legal responsibility to the organization.
13. The board understands and accepts responsibility (legal, moral, and ethical) for the actions of all employees in the organization.
14. The organization operates in accordance with its legal authority.
15. The board members act as trustees of the organization on behalf of the community at large.
16. Policies and procedures are in place to deal with ethical issues such as conflicts of interest.

Board Policies and Procedures

17. Governance structures within the board are clear (chair's or mayor's role, committee roles, staff and board roles).
18. Board meetings serve a useful purpose.
19. Board meetings are managed effectively.
20. The board chair or mayor effectively facilitates board discussions.
21. There is a clear protocol for how issues get on the agenda.
22. The board and manager ensure that meeting agendas are structured to keep the focus on priority issues.
23. Agenda items reflect important issues for the organization and the community rather than narrow interests of some board members.
24. The board provides adequate time for public input at meetings.
25. There is adequate public participation in the selection of committee and advisory-board membership.
26. The board pays as much attention to how decisions are made as it does to the final conclusion.
27. The board faithfully discloses information to the public.
28. Board policies are communicated effectively.
29. The board has written rules for how it governs the municipality or county.
30. Board policies are documented and available to every board member.

31. The board has a defined process to identify major changes needed to improve organizational leadership, structures, programs, or resources.
32. The board has an annual calendar of meetings.
33. The board has a process for handling urgent matters between meetings.

Working with Others

Items focus on how board members interact with one another, professional staff, and community stakeholders.

Interactions on the Board

34. When a new member joins the board, someone serves as a mentor to help the person learn the ropes.
35. Relationships between board members are characterized by openness, trust, and mutual respect.
36. When conflicts arise between elected officials, they are generally acknowledged and dealt with in an open, positive manner.
37. Adequate time and energy is devoted to getting every board member's input.
38. The board often requests that a decision be postponed until more information is available rather than making a decision with incomplete information.
39. Disagreements are more often resolved by discussion than by a vote.
40. Board members try to reach consensus.
41. Individual members avoid unduly consuming meeting time.
42. Members are attuned to the subtleties of issues.
43. The board operates as an effective team.
44. Members have common expectations about behavior.
45. Members communicate openly with each other.
46. Members feel safe expressing controversial views.
47. Members avoid over-politicizing the public process.
48. The organization succeeds because of the contributions and leadership of many people rather than a few.
49. The board recognizes special events in the lives of its members.
50. It is rewarding to be a part of the board.

Interactions with Staff

51. Relationships between board members, the manager, and staff are characterized by openness, trust, and mutual respect.
52. The organization attracts and retains competent and motivated people.
53. Members of the board and senior staff are comfortable managing change.
54. The board and staff work as a team to plan and manage change.
55. Board members behave in a respectful manner toward staff.
56. The board understands and respects the norms of the professional staff working for the organization.
57. Board members view staff as trusted partners.
58. The governing board, as a unit, gives direction to the professional staff.
59. The governing body gives adequate consideration to staff recommendations.
60. The staff has adequate opportunity to participate in the governing board's meetings.
61. Training and development opportunities for staff are included in the annual budget.
62. The board periodically requests information on the morale of the professional staff.
63. The board delegates operation of the local government to the manager.
64. Board members view the manager as a credible, professional leader.
65. Roles and expectations of the manager are clearly defined and communicated.
66. The manager has an opportunity to provide input during the decision-making process.
67. There is an open and honest relationship between the governing board and the manager.
68. The organization has committees that include professional staff and board members.
69. There is at least as much dialogue between board members as there is between members and management.

Interactions with Community Members

70. The local government works effectively with other organizations, businesses, and groups in the community.

71. The board seeks information and advice from leaders of other local governments and related organizations.
72. The board listens to stakeholders with diverse views, opinions, and experiences.
73. Relationships between board members and members of the public are characterized by openness, trust, and mutual respect.
74. If the board thinks a key constituency or stakeholder group may disagree with an issue it is considering, it will make an effort to hear from the group directly before taking action.
75. Board members are active and effective in representing the community's interests.
76. The board appoints members of the public, staff members, and other stakeholders, as appropriate, to committees and advisory boards.
77. Advisory-committee membership is based on the ability to serve the community rather than on personal friendships.
78. The board gives sufficient weight and attention to recommendations of advisory committees.

Making Decisions and Setting Direction

Items address the board's responsibility to set goals, clarify values and priorities, and maintain a long-term vision for the organization and the community.

Quality Decision-Making

79. Board members are open to making decisions that are creative and may present some level of risk.
80. The governing board is able to make hard choices and politically unpopular decisions when necessary.
81. The board does not attempt to avoid issues that are ambiguous or complicated.
82. The board examines the pros and cons of decisions it is about to make.
83. When faced with a complex issue, the board often brainstorms to generate a list of creative options or solutions.
84. All of the board's decisions relate to the mission of the local government.
85. The board makes every effort to take action before an issue becomes urgent or critical.

Developing Goals, Priorities, and Long-Term Vision

86. The local government's vision, mission, and values drive the decisions and choices the board makes.
87. The board has a common vision and shared goals.
88. The board's roles, such as focusing on policy and long-term planning, are defined and respected.
89. The board and staff have a systematic process for setting strategic goals and objectives that reflect their mission and vision for the future.
90. The board sets the right balance between long-term vision and immediate needs.
91. The board considers the long-term-planning priorities of the organization when dealing with policy issues.
92. Goals established by the board are realistic and doable within the stated time frame.
93. At least once a year, the board asks for the local government manager's vision for the future and strategies for achieving it.

Linking the Organization to the Community

94. Board meetings focus on important community matters.
95. The board discusses events and trends in the larger environment that may present opportunities or challenges for the local government and community.
96. The board spends time discussing issues of importance to the community's future.
97. The board often discusses where the local government and community should be in five or ten years.

Providing Resources

Items address the board's oversight and allocation of resources to achieve organizational goals and priorities.

98. The board takes a lead role in setting expectations for financial management.
99. The board ensures that adequate financial tools and resources are in place for the organization to accomplish strategic objectives.
100. The board is responsible for ensuring that finances are closely related to performance expectations and the local government's mission.

101. The board understands the local government's financial resources and makes sound decisions to prioritize spending.
102. The board has clear financial policies and procedures in place.
103. The board has a policy for handling adjustments and revisions to the budget.
104. The board avoids unbudgeted appropriations.
105. The board avoids changing the budget after its adoption except in emergencies or to handle unforeseen situations.
106. The board approves specific targets and limits on things such as debt, liquidity, and other financial ratios to warn of poor financial performance.
107. The board makes sure that the organization has the necessary tools and resources in place to manage its employees.
108. The board supports professional development for the public manager and employees.
109. Costs and benefits of services are analyzed, and that analysis is provided to the community and service users.

Accountability

Items relate to how the board maintains transparency, responsiveness, and accountability.

Accountability to the Public

110. Board members effectively represent the organization in community settings.
111. The public is adequately informed about the board's goals.
112. The board engages people from within the organization as well as outside to address the needs of the community.
113. There is adequate opportunity for a cross-section of the public to participate in the budget process.
114. The board regularly seeks feedback from a wide range of community members on the quality and effectiveness of the services they receive.
115. The local government's mission, vision, and values are reflected in the organization's reports, publications, and website.

Accountability to the Organization

116. The board receives regular (monthly or quarterly) reports on finance/budget and program performance.
117. The board reviews financial statements of expenditures and revenues against an approved budget monthly.
118. The board regularly reviews and discusses reports that provide performance data on programs and services, using comparable performance data where available.
119. The board regularly evaluates the organization's services and activities.
120. The board provides annual feedback on the manager's performance.
121. The board's policies fairly compensate the manager for good performance.
122. The governing board considers the effects of changing priorities on staff time.
123. The whole organization continuously challenges itself to improve.

Accountability as a Board

124. The board has adopted explicit goals for itself that are distinct from the goals for the organization.
125. Governing board members participate in implementing goals once they are established.
126. The board regularly monitors and evaluates progress toward strategic goals and program performance.
127. The board establishes reasonable time frames for accomplishing assignments.
128. Recommendations from evaluations and feedback are used for planning and performance improvement.
129. The board has a retreat or special session at least every two years that includes a discussion of its performance and how well it is governing.
130. The board acknowledges its responsibility for poor decisions.

Sources Used in Compiling List of Board-Evaluation Items—All Useful References for Governing Boards

Barrett, Katherine, and Richard Greene. "Short on Oversight." *Governing* (May 2006): 80.

Bluestein, Frayda S., and David M. Lawrence. *Open Meetings and Local Governments in North Carolina*, 8th ed. School of Government, 2017.

Brown, William A. "Exploring the Association Between Board and Organizational Performance in Nonprofit Organizations." *Nonprofit Management and Leadership* 15, no. 3 (2005): 317–39.

Duca, Diane J. *Nonprofit Boards: Roles, Responsibilities and Performance.* John Wiley and Sons, Inc., 1996.

Dunn, Delmer D., and Jerome S. Legge Jr. "Accountability and Responsibility of Local Government Administrators." In *The Future of Local Government Administration*, edited by H. George Frederickson and John Nalbandian. ICMA, 2002.

Fisher, Roger, and Scott Brown. *Getting Together: Building Relationships as We Negotiate.* Houghton Mifflin, 1988.

Fisher, Roger, and Daniel Shapiro. *Beyond Reason: Using Emotions as You Negotiate.* Penguin, 2005.

Gabris, Gerald T., and Kimberly L. Nelson. "Transforming Municipal Boards into Accountable, High-Performing Teams: Toward a Diagnostic Model of Governing Board Effectiveness." *Public Performance and Management Review* 36, no. 3 (2013): 472–95.

Herman, Robert D., and David O. Renz, "Board Practices of Especially Effective and Less Effective Local Nonprofit Organizations." *American Review of Public Administration* 30, no. 2 (2000): 146–60.

Holland, Thomas P. "Self-Assessment by Nonprofit Boards." *Nonprofit Management and Leadership* 2, no. 1 (1991): 25–36.

Ingley, Coral B., and Nicholas T. Van der Walt. "The Strategic Board: The Changing Role of Directors in Developing and Maintaining Corporate Capability." *Corporate Governance* 9, no. 3 (2001): 174–85.

International City/County Management Association. *Manager Evaluations Guide*. ICMA, June 2025. https://icma.org/documents/icma-manager -evaluations-guide.

Keen, Dan. "A Better Way: The Facilitated CAO Performance Review." *PM Magazine*, August 2022. https://icma.org/articles/pm-magazine/better -way-facilitated-cao-performance-review.

McLaughlin, Christopher B., ed. *County and Municipal Government in North Carolina*. 2025 ed. School of Government, 2025.

Newell, Charldean, ed. *The Effective Local Government Manager*. ICMA, 2004.

Perkins, Jan. "Case Study: It's (Gulp) Evaluation Time." *PM Magazine*, July 2005. http://icma.org/Documents/Document/Document/3602.

Schwarz, Roger, Anne Davidson, Peg Carlson, and Sue McKinney. *The Skilled Facilitator Fieldbook: Tips, Tools, and Tested Methods for Consultants, Facilitators, Managers, Trainers, and Coaches*. Jossy-Bass, 2005.

Svara, James H. "Contributions of the City Council to Effective Governance." *Popular Government* 51, no. 4 (1986): 1–8.

Tomey, Edward J. *Nonprofit Board Self-Assessment Guidebook*. Antioch University New England, 1995.

Walker, Larry W. "Governing Board, Know Thyself: Self-Assessment Is the Basis for High Performance." *Trustee* 52, no. 8 (1999): 15–19.

Appendix C.
Sample Manager Evaluation

Local Government Manager Performance Evaluation Overview

Evaluation period: _____

Evaluation Criteria

This evaluation model presents ten categories of evaluation criteria. Each category contains a statement to describe a behavior standard in that category. For each statement, the elected official will use the following scale to indicate a rating for the manager's performance.

- **5 = High satisfaction** (almost always exceeds the performance standard)
- **4 = Above-average satisfaction** (generally exceeds the performance standard)
- **3 = Average satisfaction** (generally meets the performance standard)
- **2 = Below-average satisfaction** (usually does not meet the performance standard)
- **1 = Low satisfaction** (rarely meets the performance standard)

This evaluation form also contains a provision for entering open-ended comments, including responses to specific questions and any observations you believe appropriate and pertinent to the rating period.

Timeline

Date	Activity
	Manager submits to Mayor and Council key performance highlights and accomplishments from the prior year. (Note: these should be based on a set of criteria established by the manager, mayor, and council the prior year.)
	Mayor and Council complete evaluation form using survey software and the criteria below.
	Mayor and Council conduct performance review with Manager in closed session. Determine performance rating, decide key goals for next rating period, and report rating and any compensation adjustments to Manager.

Performance Category Scoring

1. Leadership and Governing-Body Relations

- Demonstrates a nonpartisan approach that supports the success of the mayor and council.
- Builds trust through respect, honesty, collaboration, and transparency.
- Treats the mayor and council fairly, equitably, and constructively.
- Works effectively with the mayor and council to identify issues, define problems, and develop practical solutions.
- Provides timely and appropriate communication on major projects, initiatives, and critical incidents.
- Collaborates with the mayor and council to establish strategic priorities that advance the organization and community.
- Prepares council-retreat, business-meeting, and workshop agendas that encourage information sharing, informed decision-making, and efficient use of time.

2. Organizational Management

- Provides effective leadership to departments and ensures effective organizational management.
- Communicates clearly and consistently across the organization.
- Facilitates organizational change to improve productivity and performance.
- Remains informed on best practices in local government and adapts them appropriately.

3. Strategic Thinking and Future Planning

- Demonstrates strategic thinking in decision-making.
- Anticipates challenges and proactively presents solutions.
- Identifies opportunities to position the community for long-term success and investment.
- Encourages innovation and creative approaches to problem-solving.
- Assists the council in addressing future needs and developing plans for long-term trends.

4. Community Relations

- Treats community members with respect and professionalism.
- Shows dedication to serving the community and its citizens.
- Engages with residents to understand concerns and interests.
- Strives to maintain high levels of public satisfaction with services.
- Maintains a visible and appropriate presence in the community.
- Avoids unnecessary controversy and promotes constructive dialogue.
- Collaborates effectively with other local governments, state and federal agencies, and other governmental entities.

5. Fiscal Management

- Prepares a balanced, strategic budget that aligns with council priorities and service expectations.
- Maximizes the efficient and effective use of available funds.
- Presents budget recommendations in a clear, accessible format.
- Monitors and manages fiscal activities responsibly.
- Ensures long-term financial sustainability and strength for operations and infrastructure investments.

6. Narrative Evaluation

1. Describe areas where the manager demonstrated significant success over the past year.
2. Identify areas that presented challenges and may require improvement.
3. Outline key goals or areas of emphasis for the manager in the upcoming year.
4. Provide any additional comments or observations.

Appendix D.
Governing-Board Quick-Scan

Use this quick-scan to identify your board's strengths and areas for improvement in preparation for a more in-depth board evaluation. This instrument is not intended to serve as a substitute for a full board evaluation but rather to help the board determine what issues members feel need attention.

Scoring Key
SD (Strongly Disagree) = 1   **D** (Disagree) = 2   **A** (Agree) = 3   **SA** (Strongly Agree) = 4

Governing-Board Quick-Scan	SD	D	A	SA
Board members receive an orientation and training on their roles and responsibilities.	1	2	3	4
Board members operate within their legal authority.	1	2	3	4
Board members demonstrate commitment to this organization's mission and values.	1	2	3	4
This board has a systematic process for setting strategic goals and objectives that reflect our mission and vision for the future.	1	2	3	4
This board's ability to govern effectively is not impaired by conflict among its members.	1	2	3	4
This board's meetings are well-managed.	1	2	3	4
This board uses sound decision-making methods (focused on board-level issues, factual information, efficient use of time, effective implementation).	1	2	3	4
This board has adopted explicit goals for itself that are distinct from the goals for the organization.	1	2	3	4

Governing-Board Quick-Scan	SD	D	A	SA
All board members can distinguish between their own and the manager's roles and responsibilities, and they respect those distinctions.	1	2	3	4
There is a productive working relationship (good communication and mutual respect) between members of the board and the organization's manager.	1	2	3	4
The board makes sure that adequate financial resources are in place for the organization to be viable and stable and accomplish strategic objectives.	1	2	3	4
This board does a good job evaluating the performance of the manager (measuring results based on clear objectives).	1	2	3	4
This board could effectively manage any organizational crisis that might reasonably be anticipated.	1	2	3	4
This board and organization have a good balance between organizational stability and innovation.	1	2	3	4
This board has high credibility with key stakeholders (voters, community leaders, staff, and partner organizations).	1	2	3	4
Column totals				
Total for all 15 items				
Overall score (Total divided by 15)				

Scoring Key:
SD (Strongly Disagree) = 1   **D** (Disagree) = 2   **A** (Agree) = 3   **SA** (Strongly Agree) = 4